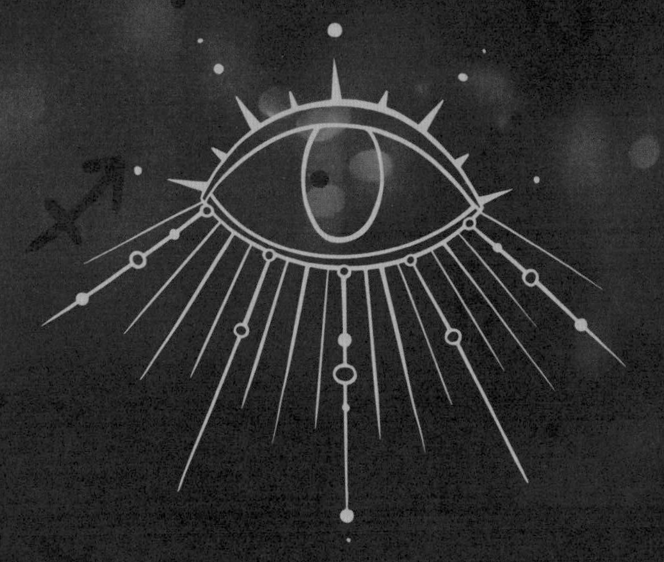

# SPELLCRAFT

## A GUIDED JOURNAL FOR CASTING, CLEANSING & BLESSING

# CONTENTS

# WELCOME, WITCHES

What is a spell? A turn of phrase, a few components, the feeling of something well crafted? The truth is that if it's your spell, it can be defined as any of these things (or anything you want, for that matter).

In the case of this journal, crystals, burnables, and other physical aspects of spells are all paid homage, but words are what really have the power here—power that *you* give them by bringing them into the world.

A lot of spells take time and are not just a quick wave of a wand (so to speak). Giving yourself the space and opportunity to express what you want through writing will help you channel your requests to the universe with a bit more precision. Writing will also help you, the caster, manifest your desired outcomes.

Each spell in this book either has a journal component to it or a prompt to help you more deeply internalize the desired effects of each spell. Use this journal to expand your knowledge of yourself and spellcraft as you develop as a person and a witch.

A general word of caution: These spells should never be cast for someone without their consent. Spells and witchcraft are primarily used to bring balance where there is discord. When the energy doesn't flow both ways, things could go wrong.

Within these pages are several spells to get you started, and include:

- *Poppets*
- *Knot magic*
- *Floor washes*
- *Goddess baths*
- *Candle magic*
- *Rune magic*
- *Moon magic*
- *Tarot magic*
- *Kitchen witchery*
- *Plant magic*

Spells do their hardest work when you make them yourself. Try mixing and matching components to make spells that are truly unique to your needs. A cocoon could symbolize change and be used as a component in a spell for shedding an old piece of yourself. A silver coin could symbolize a resource, whether for something as literal as financial wealth or something else entirely, such as internal motivation. Keys unlock new energies and are great for wishes.

Looking past their practical purposes, utilize symbolism and go out into the world to find magically charged objects that can help you build your own spells.

# WHEEL OF THE YEAR

# IMBOLC (CANDLEMAS)

This holiday celebrates a journey out of the dark and into the light of spring. It falls at the halfway point between the winter solstice and the spring equinox in the northern hemisphere (usually February 1, but this can fluctuate). Imbolc is a Celtic holiday that has been tied to Saint Brigid in Catholicism and can be celebrated with Brigid Crosses or Brigid Dolls to burn during the spring equinox. Here, we're replacing the Brigid Doll with a poppet of yourself to bring about positive change.

## MATERIALS

- *Pencil or pen*
- *Paper*
- *Scissors*
- *Cloth*
- *Sewing pins*
- *Sewing needle*
- *Thread*
- *Small pencil*
- *Cinnamon stick (optional)*
- *Dried mint (optional)*
- *Sea salt (optional)*
- *Dirt (optional)*
- *Cotton stuffing*

## PROCESS

1. Draw the loosest outline of a human being on a piece of paper—head, arms, body, and legs. It doesn't need to be anything fancy. You can even draw a skirt instead of individual legs. Cut out your drawing to use as a template.
2. Pin the template to the cloth with sewing pins and cut out two people to be the front and back of your poppet. You can fold the fabric over to cut out the two templates at the same time.
3. Sew the fabric pieces closed at the bottom and the top, leaving the middle open on either side so that you can fill it later.

4. With the small pencil, write good intentions, successful changes you'd like to bring into the fold, new paths, and hopes and dreams on a small piece of paper. Set aside.
5. Stuff the poppet with the remaining items to ground your poppet: Add the cinnamon stick (for fire and passion), the mint (for air and transformation), the sea salt (for water and conflict resolution), and a bit of dirt (for the earth and home). Add more of the elements that you want more of in your life. Add the paper and small pencil (if it fits), along with the cotton stuffing.
6. Stitch up the sides of the poppet and set it on your altar. Keep it on your altar until spring, and when the urge strikes you, talk to your poppet—talk to it sweetly, thank it for getting you this far, tell it the changes you're welcoming into your life.
7. When the spring equinox arrives, burn your doll in a firepit or fire-safe pot outside, releasing all of the positivity you've fed your poppet into the world. Always use caution when employing fire in your witchcraft. Keep your fingers safe and be wary of fire hazards nearby.

## WORDS OF WISDOM

DEPENDING ON WHAT CHANGES YOU'RE TRYING TO ENACT, YOU MAY BENEFIT FROM PLACING DIFFERENT ITEMS INTO YOUR POPPET (E.G., CLEAR QUARTZ AMPLIFIES MAGIC). REMAIN AWARE OF THE CAPACITY OF YOUR POPPET (AND YOURSELF) AND TRY NOT TO OVERSTUFF IT, AS DOING THIS CAN CAUSE THE SPELL TO LOSE ITS POTENCY.

To find positivity and change, it often helps to show gratitude for how far we've come. Spend 10 minutes writing about what you're grateful for.

Change is ambiguous. Write down all the different changes you could bring into your life. This is a creative exercise, so these changes can be large or small, grand or miniscule. You will use them in your next prompt.

Focus on two to five of the positive changes from the previous journal entry that you could employ in your life. What would these changes mean realistically for you? Do you need anything to make them happen? Pick at least one simple and one outrageous change.

# SPRING EQUINOX (OSTARA)

During the spring, or vernal, equinox, the German goddess Ostara (Eostre), from which Easter owes its name, is paid tribute. The spring equinox (usually March 21, but this can fluctuate) revolves around fertility, new growth, total balance between day and night, and the emergence from a cold winter. This ritual can be performed at dawn, solar noon, or sunset, or any combination of the three. If outside, etch a circle in the ground, ideally in fresh dirt, in a place where you can watch the sun's journey across the sky.

## MATERIALS

- *Stick (if outside) or piece of chalk (if inside)*
- *Yard of string*
- *Small white candle*
- *Small yellow candle*
- *Small green candle*
- *Small black candle*
- *Small blue candle*
- *Small pink candle*
- *Floral essential oil (e.g., lavender, rose, geranium)*
- *Earthy essential oil (e.g., cedar, sage, frankincense)*

## PROCESS

1. Tie the stick (if outside) or chalk (if inside) to one end of the string. Anchor the other end of the string to where you want the center of the circle to be. With that end solidly secured, use the other end as a compass to draw a perfect circle in the dirt or on the floor.
2. Face east (the direction of the rising sun) and place the white candle directly in front of you. If your circle were a clock, this white candle would be 12. Place the yellow candle where 1 would be, the green where 5 would be, the black where 6 would be, the blue where 7 would be, and the pink where 11 would be.

*(continued)*

3. Anoint the white candle with the floral essential oil, using your finger to smear a small amount of the oil on the candle while saying, "As above."
4. Anoint the black candle with the earthy essential oil while saying, in the same way you anointed the white, "So below."
5. Light the black candle and say, "As without."
6. Light the white candle and say, "So within."
7. If completing the ritual in one sitting, repeat the phrases above with all the candles of opposing colors: yellow and blue, pink and green. If completed at dawn, noon, and dusk, pick pairs of candles to light for each of your sittings.
8. Whether in one sitting or over a few sittings, meditate on the nature of light and dark while watching the fire burn down the candles. If you wish to complete the spell before the candles burn out, use a snuffer, if possible, to extinguish the candle.
9. If returning to the ritual once or twice during the day, try to light the same number of candles each time. Seek symmetry if possible. And face the sun (without looking directly at it).

## WORDS OF WISDOM

FIRE IS A POWERFUL ELEMENT. USE CAUTION AND WEAR CLOTHES THAT WON'T BILLOW IN THE BREEZE TO AVOID ACCIDENTS. ALWAYS BE AWARE OF WHERE IT'S BURNING AND IF THERE ARE ANY FIRE HAZARDS NEARBY. KEEP A PITCHER OF WATER OR A FIRE EXTINGUISHER HANDY IF YOU'RE PRONE TO ACCIDENTS.

Light and dark are never simply good and bad. To focus on balance, write about traditionally light things that may be considered "bad" and what beneficial things happen in the dark.

When has the darkness served you? When has the darkness scared you, and what specifically about it made you feel that way?

How has the light served you? How do you keep your own fire burning when resources are low?

# BELTANE (MAY EVE)

Occurring on April 30, Beltane is when your transitional energy is at its height. The seeds have been planted, the ideas are growing, and this holiday is about keeping momentum. For this spell, we'll be making a pentagram and charging it with a crystal. There are many different pentagrams that you can buy, but making your own pentagram will supercharge your magic for the rest of the year.

## MATERIALS

- *Pen or pencil*
- *Paper*
- *Twine*
- *5 twigs from different trees, all roughly the same length*
- *Clear quartz crystal*

## PROCESS

1. Draw a pentagram on a piece of paper as a template and place the five twigs atop it in the shape of the star.
2. Starting at the top of the star, tie the points together using the twine. Cross the tip first, circling the twine twice to make sure it's firmly secured. Then thread either end of the twine between the twigs and over the top, tying it tightly in a knot to tie them into a V shape.
3. Repeat this around the circle, tying each point off as you go.
4. Place your pentagram on your altar with the clear quartz crystal in the center to assist in any future spells you craft.

## WORDS OF WISDOM

SPRIGS OF FRESH HERBS ARE GOOD ALTERNATIVES TO TWIGS IF YOU LIVE IN AN URBAN AREA AND CAN FIND THEM AT A GROCERY STORE OR FARMERS' MARKET. THYME, ROSEMARY, SAGE, OREGANO, AND BASIL WILL DRY TO A SLIGHTLY WOODY TEXTURE.

May Day is all about activism. What areas of your community are you most excited to bring your light to and how are you going to do so?

The pentagram is a distinct pagan symbol. What does being a witch mean to you? What do you intend to use your homemade pentagram for in the future?

If this isn't the first spell you've cast, how has your understanding of witchcraft changed? If it is your first cast spell, congratulations! What emotions did it stir?

# SUMMER SOLSTICE (LITHA)

The summer solstice (usually June 21, but this can fluctuate) is the longest day of the year and draws most of it practices from the sun. Having a bonfire or hosting a barbecue are great ways to pay tribute to the burning ball of gas in the sky, but for more of a slow burn, try this recipe for making your own incense. These small, aromatic cones are great to light on your own in an incense holder or to throw into a bonfire. You will need to start this process a week before the summer solstice.

## MATERIALS

- *1 teaspoon dried lavender flowers*
- *Mortar and pestle*
- *Bowl*
- *1 teaspoon dried chamomile flowers*
- *About 10 dried rose petals*
- *1 teaspoon makko powder*
- *Distilled water*
- *Eyedropper*
- *Parchment paper*

## PROCESS

1. Add the dried lavender to your mortar and pestle. Grind the dried flowers into a fine powder. If you have a coffee grinder that is ONLY used for herbs, this may also be used to make the process faster. Place the lavender powder into a bowl.
2. Repeat the first step with the chamomile and rose petals and add these powders to the bowl with the ground lavender.
3. Add the makko powder to the bowl with the herbs. Let the powders sit overnight so that they can incorporate.
4. The next day, add the distilled water, drop by drop with the eyedropper, until the powders turn into a thick paste that resembles wet sand. Ten drops or less should be sufficient, but add as much water as you need to get the powders to hold their form.

5. Using your fingers, form the mixture into about five small cones that are each no more than 1 inch (2.5 cm) tall. Place the cones, bases down, on a piece of parchment paper and let them dry for at least two days. After the first day, tip the cones over so that the bases can dry.
6. On the summer solstice at high noon, when the sun is centered in the sky, light up the incense cones in an incense dish and ruminate on what feeds your fire. If you had a hard time forming cones, fill a fireproof pot with salt, place your incense powder in the center, and light it with a grill lighter. The mixture should still burn aromatically.

---

## WORDS OF WISDOM

TRADE OUT ANY OF THE FLOWERS FOR A DIFFERENT TYPE OF DRIED FLOWER, BUT MAKE SURE YOU USE MAKKO POWDER, BECAUSE THAT IS THE BINDING AGENT THAT HOLDS THE CONES TOGETHER.

---

Summer solstice rituals were performed to gain favor with the gods and reap a bountiful harvest. What goals do you have in motion that could be completed by the time autumn arrives?

Fire and the sun burn passionately. What are some things that set your body and spirit alight?

When burning your incense (especially if you made substitutions to the flowers), what associations does the aroma bring about? Any memories? Feelings? Good vibes?

# LUGHNASADH (LAMMAS)

Occurring halfway between the summer solstice and the autumn equinox (traditionally it occurs on August 1), this holiday celebrates the first crops of the harvest. The name is derived from the Celtic god Lugh, who is considered the Celtic counterpart to Hermes/Mercury. If you bake, now is an excellent time to start baking bread in honor of the impending harvest. If you're not particularly good at baking, this spell is the prefect introduction to kitchen witchery.

## MATERIALS

- *Heatproof bowl*
- *3 tablespoons red pepper flakes*
- *2 whole dried chile peppers*
- *1¼ cups (300 ml) vegetable oil, such as canola*
- *2 thin medallions fresh ginger*
- *Saucepan*
- *Mason jar*
- *Sieve*
- *Funnel*
- *Favorite crusty bread loaf, ideally circular in shape*
- *Salt, to taste*
- *Basting brush (optional)*

## PROCESS

1. In a heatproof bowl, add the red pepper flakes and whole dried chiles. Set aside.
2. Add the oil and ginger to a saucepan over medium-low heat. Do NOT overheat the oil. Cook for about 5 minutes, until the oil reaches about 180°F (82°C).
3. Carefully pour the oil and ginger over the red pepper flakes and dried chiles. Allow to cool to room temperature for at least 2 hours.
4. Strain the oil into the jar using the sieve and funnel. The oil is ready to serve, but if you'd like it to be spicier, place the whole chiles in the jar and keep in the refrigerator. This oil infusion will keep in the refrigerator for about a month.

*(continued)*

5. If gathering with friends, put the oil out with sliced bread for dipping, adding salt to taste. If enjoying on your own, use the basting brush to draw symbols of abundance on the bread. These can be runes, drawings, or abstract imagery. Sprinkle salt on top of the loaf to break bread with a higher power. Eat and give thanks for all that you have been gifted.

## WORDS OF WISDOM

BREAKING BREAD AND THE HARVEST REPRESENT CONNECTING WITH FRIENDS, FAMILY, AND FOUND FAMILY. HOST A GATHERING OR SEEK OUT INDIVIDUALS WHO WARM YOUR HEART.

Have you partaken in kitchen witchery before? How do you associate the home and hearth with your craft?

This ritual can be used to “break bread” with the gods. What deities do you identify with?

How is your harvest shaping up to be? Now is a good time to check back in with your New Year's resolutions to see how you're faring. What stagnant passions do you wish to reignite?

# AUTUMNAL EQUINOX (MABON)

Much of the wheel of the year has been focused on bringing more light into the fold. As the autumnal equinox (usually September 21, but this can fluctuate) beckons the cold, dark months of winter, it's important to not only seek out the light, but also to acknowledge our shadows. Getting to know the darker parts of yourself—personal traits or tendencies that you are not proud of but that are still a part of you—is an important path toward shadow work. The best time to start is when you still have the light of the sun to guide you.

## MATERIALS

- *Athame or needle*
- *3 to 5 tealights*
- *Paper and pen*
- *Small paring knife or vegetable peeler*
- *Crayons in 3 to 5 colors*

## PROCESS

1. Look upon the runes on page 34 with a soft gaze and try to pick one or two runes that call to you on their appearance alone, without thinking too hard about what they mean. These runes will be ones that you might not even realize you need but that your subconscious will illuminate for you.
2. Read their meanings and pick three or four that call to your conscious mind.
3. While thinking about what these runes mean to you, carefully use the athame or needle to carve a rune into the wax of a tealight (one rune per tealight), minding your fingers. The grooves do not have to be deep. Write the runes down on a separate piece of paper so that you can reference them later after the spell is complete.
4. Minding the wicks, use a paring knife to carefully shave a different crayon onto each of the tealights, picking the color that best suits your rune. Record which color corresponds to which rune on the separate piece of paper.

5. Light each candle, one by one, saying the rune name and what it can bring to you and your practice.
6. Sit in the light of your candles, observing the flames as they burn down and the wax claims the runes. The colors of the crayon wax will help you identify which candles correspond to which runes as the fire melts the marks carved in the wax.
7. What do you see in the fire? How do the shadows dance behind the flames? What parts of you burn brightest? What is the flickering darkness hiding? Ponder these questions and begin to think about what your own shadow holds.

---

## WORDS OF WISDOM

USE THIS SPACE HONESTLY AND OPENLY. IF YOUR SUBCONSCIOUS PICKS RUNES THAT YOU CANNOT IMAGINE BEING USEFUL TO YOU, USE THIS TIME TO FIND CREATIVE WAYS TO CONNECT YOUR CONSCIOUS AND UNCONSCIOUS MIND. PERHAPS YOU PICKED *HAGALAZ* AND CAN'T THINK OF A PAST PATTERN THAT ISN'T SERVING YOU. OR YOU PICKED *INGUZ* BUT ARE FEELING LONELY AS OPPOSED TO NEEDING SPACE. IF YOU CAN, TRY TO REFRAME THE WAY YOU'RE LOOKING AT YOUR PROBLEMS TO FIND ALTERNATIVE SOLUTIONS.

---

# RUNES

**FEHU:** luck, wealth, prosperity, beginnings

**URUZ:** strength, self-control, dominion

**THURISAZ:** resistance, defense, protection

**ANSUZ:** old gods, divinity, inheritance, listening, wisdom

**RAIDO:** journey as the destination, direction, adventure

**KENAZ:** creativity, passion, enlightenment

**GEBO:** talent, gift, sacrifice

**WUNJO:** joy, peace, success, happiness, temporary fulfillment

**HAGALAZ:** confrontation of the past, patterns, flow of energy

**NAUTHIZ:** necessity, warnings, acting improperly

**ISA:** stasis, stillness, ego, self

**JERA:** seasons, cycles, change, fruition

**EIHWAZ:** trust, teamwork, friends

**PERTHRO:** mystery, occult, serendipity

**ALGIZ:** high vibes, spiritual awareness, protection, fate

**SOWULO:** extreme strength, light, energy

**TEIWAZ:** justice, morality, honor

**BERKANA:** growth and rebirth

**EHWAZ:** collaboration, harmony, common goals

**MANNAZ:** humankind, awareness, balance between the mind-body-soul

**LAGUZ:** collective memory, dreams, unconscious

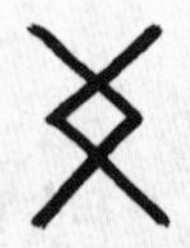

**INGUZ:** process, internal growth, resting, biding your time

**DAGAZ:** dawn, day, personal fulfillment

**OTHILA:** solid, immovable, loyalty

Runes are ancient Norse symbols used for divination that still call to modern practitioners. Which runes interest you? Are there some that seem to tell you a story with their shapes and meanings?

Describe the shadows you saw in your runic candles. What shapes did they have? Did they remind you of anything? Did some of your runes cause the flames to dance particularly wildly?

Have you named any of your shadows? It can be something creative, like "Nighthawk," or something less abstract, like "Social Anxiety." Use the space below to explore what you consider to be the darker parts of yourself.

# SAMHAIN (HALLOWE'EN)

Samhain is traditionally observed from the evening of October 31 to the evening of November 1. By creating a King of Winter or Crone of Winter, or both, out of the dead leaves and bramble you find in your yard, you can symbolically offer the dead a place at your table. Once you have acquired a seven-day candle for this spell, go out into the yard and collect all manner of dead plants—sticks, leaves, corn husks, dried flowers—anything you can find and fashion into the shape of a man (the King of Winter) or a woman (the goddess in her Crone form).

## MATERIALS

- *Yard clippings*
- *Twine*
- *Seven-day white candle*

## PROCESS

1. Any image will work for fashioning your king or crone, but an easy way to start is by first making a cross with sticks and then tying more pieces to the form with twine as you go. Give them arms and legs, or a skirt, tying the pieces to your cross with twine.
2. Make your king or crone outside so that when you are done, you can welcome them into the house with you. Light the candle in the window to guide your ancestors to the vessel you have made for them. Light the candle when you arrive home every day and snuff it before you go to bed every night. Depending on how long you burn the candle each day, it could last anywhere from one to two weeks. Do NOT leave it unattended, seeing as it could attract anything.
3. Place your king or crone on the kitchen table and share a cup of tea or wine with them. Keep them until the spring equinox, when you can burn them in a bonfire in the hopes that a plentiful harvest (or just good tidings) will come in the following year.

The king stands for the cold necessity of winter. He calls to us to be strong and have faith that the warmer weather and longer hours in the sun will return. What did you harvest this year that will warm you throughout winter?

The triple goddess in neo-paganism assumes three forms: the maiden, who is only at the start of her ventures; the mother, who is stable and full of power, fertility, and life; and the crone, who is symbolic of endings and the wisdom that comes with age. What have you learned this year that you think you will carry on?

Samhain is when the veil between the worlds of the living and the dead is at its thinnest. If you could speak to your ancestors, what aspects of their wisdom would you be most interested in knowing? Which living relatives would you like to gather knowledge from during this time?

# WINTER SOLSTICE (YULE)

The winter solstice (usually December 21, but this can fluctuate) is the shortest day of the year, and Yule symbolizes that even during the darkest days, the sun will still return to us. It's a time for reflection and to focus on the things that really matter. Traditional witchery would have you light a Yule log decorated with a wreath and other burnables while meditating on what will bring you the most happiness (and light) for the rest of the cold winter. However, if you can't burn a log due to where you live, an alternative is to have a Yule altar.

## MATERIALS

- *Wide cylindrical log (birch, oak, or pine, sourced ethically and early)*
- *Rosemary*
- *Sage*
- *Lavender*
- *Tealights*
- *Athame or needle*
- *Red candle*
- *Green candle*
- *White candle*

## PROCESS

1. Find a corner of your home to lay out your sacred space. This is *your* altar, so arrange your materials in whatever way brings you the most joy. Some ideas include setting them up in the symbol of a star, pentagram, heart, sun, or any other symbol that will work.
2. Lay out your herbs.
3. Use an athame or needle to carve the word of a thing that you're grateful for into each of the three candles. If the candles are small, symbols can work as well.
4. Once your Yule altar is decorated, keep it in a safe space out of reach of familiars and children. Make note of your favorite things to add to your altar next year in the material section above to help build your practice over time.
5. On the day of the winter solstice (it changes from year to year), light the candles and fill out the following journal pages.

Yule is a time for reflecting on the previous year and to ruminate on how the darkest nights can bring us some of our warmest memories. What are some warm memories that you wish to remember and cherish?

Reflect on the light you have experienced and write about the joys you hope to draw into the coming year.

What are some things you can leave in the past year and how will doing this create space in your life?

# CREATIVITY & CREATION

# CANDLE MAGIC FOR CREATIVITY

Creative endeavors are brought about by the most passionate parts of us. This easy candle spell harnesses the power of fire to help you unlock inspiration. This spell is most powerful right when you light the candle and can encourage a couple of hours of creative work. Lighting the candle at the beginning of the week or during the waxing moon will help you make the most of the next week or moon cycle.

## MATERIALS

- *Athame*
- *Yellow candle*
- *Basil essential oil*

## PROCESS

1. Use your athame to carve the *Kenaz* rune (see page 34) onto your candle. *Kenaz* is the rune for knowledge and torch bearing, so it should magnify your creative energies. Aside from the sigil, feel free to carve in any symbols or words you draw power from in your craft.
2. Once you've carved your candle, using your finger, anoint the etchings with the essential oil.
3. Light the candle, and while it burns, use the energy of the flame to help inspire your work.

---

## WORDS OF WISDOM

IN CANDLE MAGIC, IT IS ADVISED THAT YOU EXTINGUISH THE CANDLES EITHER WITH A SNUFFER OR BY USING WET FINGERS. THAT BEING SAID, IF YOU DO NOT FEEL COMFORTABLE PUTTING OUT A CANDLE WITH YOUR FINGERS (YOU NEED THOSE, AFTER ALL!), BLOWING OUT THE CANDLE IS ALWAYS ACCEPTABLE.

---

What are some challenges that you've come across in your creative process? How would you talk a friend through said problems?

Another way to unlock creativity for more difficult projects is to give yourself space to create something in a judgment-free environment. Use these pages to create a poem, write a short story, or journal your insight into a current observation about the world around you to help spark your potential.

Fear squanders creativity unless you harness it and incorporate it into whatever grand creation you're working on. How can you incorporate your fears or doubts into what you're making so that it is a cathartic experience?

# INCENSE RITUAL FOR DIFFICULT TASKS

Burning the candle at both ends is ill-advised, but if you struggle with focusing on difficult tasks, tying them to a timer, such as burning incense, can help ignite your creative fire and keep it smoldering long after the incense has burned out.

## MATERIALS

- *Pack of your favorite incense*
- *Candle or lighter*
- *Incense holder*

## PROCESS

1. Light the incense, ideally over an open flame, and wait until it catches.
2. Allow the incense to burn as if it's a wick for about 20 seconds.
3. Let the flame extinguish and watch the smoke dance as it smolders.
4. With the incense in hand, set your intention. Focus your mind on the task at hand.
5. Place the incense in an incense holder and get to work. The aroma will follow you throughout your creative endeavor. Once the incense burns out, you can either welcome success or (more often than not) find that whatever flummoxed you before is now too enticing to stop.

---

## WORDS OF WISDOM

IF YOU DON'T HAVE AN INCENSE HOLDER, A POTTED PLANT WORKS JUST AS WELL. JUST MAKE SURE THE BURNING PART OF THE INCENSE DOESN'T TOUCH THE FOLIAGE.

---

What type of incense did you pick? What memories does its fragrance light for you?

Fire is an element of passion, but as the burning of incense shows us, passion doesn't have to be wildly out of control. Passion can be sustainable if it is rooted in balance. What are some ways you relax after chasing your ambitions?

Incense has been used in many different spiritual rituals across many different practices for over a millennium. Is this venture something you find spiritual? What do you define as a spiritual practice?

# WITCH'S LADDER

Knot magic is simple and can be hidden just about anywhere. Every strand becomes an opportunity. A loose string on your sleeve? A witch's ladder for stability. A stray hair? A witch's ladder for beauty and confidence. Are you particularly crafty with yarn or embroidery? Those projects are perfect places to hide spells in plain sight . . . if you're interested in that sort of thing.

## MATERIALS

- *Piece of string, twine, cord, or embroidery floss*

## PROCESS

1. This spell primarily comes from the caster's heart. The bones of the spell involve tying three to ten knots in a piece of string or anything that can be knotted.
2. As you tie each knot, compose a short rhyming couplet that corresponds with the spell you're casting. The more knots you tie, the more powerful the spell. Here are some samples of rhyming couplets to get you started:

By knot of one, my spell's begun
By knot of two, I see it through
By knot of three, so mote it be
By knot of four, it grows evermore
By knot of five, the spell is alive

By knot of six, my will is fixed
By knot of seven, spirits bestow their blessing
By knot of eight, 'tis tied with fate
By knot of nine, the power is mine
By knot of ten, it repeats time and again

3. As you get better at witch's ladders, come up with creative ways to personalize each ladder to whatever intention you're tying it to.

## WORDS OF WISDOM

WHEN IT COMES FROM THE HEART, IT DOESN'T HAVE TO RHYME PERFECTLY.

Try writing some witch's ladder couplets below.

Some problems are more vexing than others. Use the space below to write about a minor annoyance that might only require three knots to send off a spell.

Knots are present in our bodies too. In a quiet place, close your eyes, scan your body from your head to your toes, and find a physical knot in your body. Can you tie this feeling to an emotion or a recent experience?

# IDEAS TO SEED

Magic is the art of imbuing physical symbols with intentions to manifest our best selves. Both seeds and eggs are symbols for infinite intentions. The smallest seed can create a towering tree and an innocuous egg can grow into a kimono dragon.

## MATERIALS

- *1 eggshell (this spell works best with at least half of a large shell)*
- *Enough dirt to fill the pot (no more than 3 cups, or 260 g, is needed)*
- *Small pot*
- *Permanent marker in your favorite color*
- *Seed(s) for your favorite plant*
- *Water*
- *Patience*

## PROCESS

1. Thoroughly rinse the eggshell to remove any excess egg whites. Let the eggshell dry on the counter on a paper towel until it is no longer damp, about an hour.
2. While the egg dries, add a layer of dirt, about 1 to 2 inches (2.5 to 5 cm) thick, to the bottom of the pot and make a small divot for your eggshell.
3. Use your marker to write a single goal, ambition, or attitude onto the outside of your eggshell. Write slowly and deliberately, and paint a picture in your head about what enacting this positive change in your life would look like. Are you happier? Healthier? More fulfilled? Really think about what it would mean to you.
4. Nestle the eggshell into the nest of dirt you've made and add about a teaspoon of dirt inside of it.

*(continued)*

5. Take the recommended amount of seeds for your plant (usually one to five, depending on the variety of your plant) and hold them in your palm. Plants like it when you sweetly talk to them, so give your seeds kind intentions as you lay them into the dirt in the eggshell.
6. Gently fill the shell and the rest of the pot with dirt and lightly water it.
7. Keep the pot in direct sunlight and make a conscious effort to water it at least once a week.

## WORDS OF WISDOM

SPRING IS WHEN MOST SEEDS GROW BEST. MAKE SURE YOU SET UP YOUR SPELL FOR SUCCESS BY PICKING PLANTS THAT ARE NATIVE TO YOUR CLIMATE AND LIKELY TO GROW WITH THE AMOUNT OF SUN YOU HAVE AT YOUR DISPOSAL.

What goal are you trying to manifest? How do your seeds symbolize this goal?

Plant magic is a way for us to reconnect with Mother Earth and her magic in an age of disconnect. Where are some places you feel most rooted?

As your plant grows, make note of any unexpected opportunities that are in some way connected to the seed you've planted.

# COURAGE & HOPE

# GOOD VIBES ONLY CLEANSING BATH

Negativity is sticky, and we can carry little bits of it around without even realizing it. By consciously scrubbing them from your physical body, your spiritual body can grow and prosper.

## MATERIALS

- *1 cup (45 g) dried or fresh rue*
- *2 cups (90 g) white rose petals (or 2 cups, or 475 ml, rosewater)*
- *3 bay leaves*
- *Large bowl or bucket*
- *2 cups (475 ml) Florida water*
- *Sea salt*
- *White candle*

## PROCESS

1. Wake at dawn on the day of the new moon and begin your day in silence. Do not look at your phone, do not talk to your familiar, do not converse with housemates. Silence charges this spell and invites only your energy into it.
2. Boil a pot of water and steep the herbs for 10 minutes. If using rosewater instead of rose petals, you will add it in the next step.
3. Pour the hot water into the large bowl or bucket and add the Florida water, sea salt, and rosewater (if using). Add cool or room temperature water to the mixture until it reaches a temperature that you find comfortable to bathe in.
4. Light the candle in the bathroom and bring your bowl or bucket into the bathtub with you.
5. Wash yourself with the water. Gently scrub the herbs into your skin. Try to keep as much of the herb mixture from going down the drain after you rinse it from your body.
6. As you find the bay leaves, take a moment to hold them at three of your seats of power: Hold the first to your heart and let go of emotional labor that no longer serves you. Hold the second between your brows, on your third eye,

the seat of consciousness. Let go of any ideas or habits that you no longer wish to cling to. Place the final bay leaf on the crown of your head. Draw the crown of your head up while letting your spine hang down and fill yourself with all the hopes for what you wish to grow into.

7. Collect all the herbs from the bathtub and set them aside. Give them a second life by either disposing of them as compost or by letting them dry out and burning them.
8. Take a cold shower to remove the residue of the spell or any lingering negativity.
9. Go about your day with new energy.

---

## WORDS OF WISDOM

BATHS ARE GREAT WAYS TO HARNESS THE ANCIENT KNOWLEDGE AND POWER IN PLANTS. THEY'RE ALSO A TIME FOR PAMPERING YOURSELF, WHICH IN AND OF ITSELF IS A CLEANSING EXPERIENCE.

---

What emotions did you set free? What did they make room for?

What old ideas have you grown out of? Why are you leaving them behind?

This bath is all about kicking out the old and ushering in new energy. With new energy comes new hope. What does genuine hope feel like to you?

# KEY TO HAPPINESS

In truth, happiness is more of a journey than a destination with a locked door. However, unlocking your door and bringing down your walls so that happiness can begin to blossom is a step in the right direction. Use this spell to help open your heart for joy-filled experiences.

## MATERIALS

- *Matches*
- *Red candle*
- *Key to be used ONLY for this spell (a skeleton key is recommended)*
- *Heatproof dish or tray*
- *Tag with a ribbon tie (you can make one out of a small piece of cardstock and string)*

## PROCESS

1. Sit in a dark, quiet room with all your spell components laid out in front of you. Take a deep breath and try to extend your awareness into the shadows around you. Humans are afraid of the dark and the unknown, so this may be a bit uncomfortable.
2. Strike the match and notice the golden glow that the flame gives off. Light your candle with it and watch the fire dance on the wick for a moment.
3. Take your key and whisper your wishes to it. Be honest. Abstain from harshly judging yourself for what you want—it is okay if your desires seem selfish.
4. Hold the key over the fire, minding your fingers, and let the flames lick across the metal grooves.
5. While you watch the fire, repeat warm and kind affirmations in your head to drive off the darkness.
6. When the key becomes hot, lay it in the dish or on the tray and turn on the light.

*(continued)*

7. Write down one word that symbolizes what your key to happiness is. Use abstract language as opposed to singular things. For example, if you want a romantic relationship, perhaps write down "companionship," or if you want to be rich, write down "resources."
8. Once the key has cooled, tie the tag onto your key and place it in your pillowcase. Your dreams should aid you in your quest for happiness.

## WORDS OF WISDOM

TIE YOUR HAPPINESS ONLY TO YOURSELF. WHEN YOU INVOLVE OTHER PARTIES (THAT MAY OR MAY NOT BE WILLING), IT BECOMES HARDER TO MANIFEST. WHEN WE LOOK FOR HAPPINESS ROOTED IN OURSELVES, IT BECOMES A MORE SUSTAINABLE EMOTION.

Think of yourself as a happy child. When children's needs are met, they are blissful bundles of joy. Relive some of your happiest childhood memories and elicit similar feelings as a more complex version of yourself.

Our own mental hurdles can block us from being happy. Every day for a week, write down the first thing that comes to your mind when you wake up in the morning. By catching your mind before it's fully conscious, it will be easier for you to discern what you need to be happy.

When you're blue, it's sometimes difficult to see all the blessings you have at your disposal. Fill up each of these lines with the things you're grateful for. They can be as small as clean socks and as big as spiritual fulfillment.

# POUCHES FOR DREAMWORK

The labyrinth of our dreams is a fascinating place to get lost in. Dreamwork is a mystical process that, like the sun, is difficult to look directly at. Whether you're plagued by demons in your sleep, wish to open your mind for psychic dreams, or merely want a little help getting to sleep, these pouches will protect and guide your sleeping self into dreamland.

## MATERIALS

- *5 small drawstring pouches (preferably in purple or navy velvet)*
- *2 bowls (glass or crystal if possible)*
- *2 parts dried mugwort*
- *2 parts dried rue*
- *Lavender essential oil*
- *½ part dried lavender*
- *½ part dried jasmine*

## PROCESS

1. Set out all your ingredients and open your five drawstring pouches.
2. In one of the bowls, mix together the mugwort and the rue. This mixture protects the dreamer and opens their dreams for psychic messages. Shake a few drops of the lavender essential oil into the mixture and toss to incorporate. Fill four of the pouches with this mixture (one for each of your bedposts) and tightly tie.
3. In the second bowl, combine the dried lavender and jasmine. This aroma should be fragrant and calming. If the smell of either of the herbs does not elicit a calming reaction, omit it. Shake a few drops of the lavender essential oil into the mixture and toss to incorporate. Fill the remaining pouch (for your pillow). Tie tightly.
4. Secure the four mugwort-rue pouches to your bedposts. Place the lavender-jasmine pouch inside your pillowcase to fill your head with good dreams.
5. Every day during the week after you complete these pouches, write down what you dreamed about first thing in the morning.

Describe dreams that you've had previously. They can be overarching themes or specific details. Prime your mind for remembering dreams in this way.

Write down your first dream here. Try to scour it for details.

Once the week has passed, write down what symbols consistently showed up in your dreams, regardless of whether they seem important or not. Anything that repeats more than once is a message. If it shows up more than four times, it is an important message.

# PEACE & HARMONY

# TEA WITH THE SUN

Witches are frequently drawn to the soothing cover of darkness that accompanies the moon, but the sun has quite a lot to offer as well. The sun brings light, life, and knowledge to the world, and this spell lets you harness its energy. The sun is strongest when it crests the horizon in the morning, and this spell is most charged during a solstice or an equinox.

## MATERIALS

- *2 tablespoons loose-leaf black tea*
- *1 teaspoon dried rosehips*
- *1 teaspoon dried chamomile flowers*
- *2 cups (475 ml) cold water*
- *Clear glass bowl, jar, or pitcher*

## PROCESS

1. The day is new! Set your alarm for 30 minutes before the sun rises on the day of the solstice or equinox.
2. Combine the tea, rosehips, chamomile, and water in the bowl, jar, or pitcher, and sit outside where you can see the sunrise.
3. Make yourself comfortable before the sun begins to peek over the horizon.
4. As the light begins to touch your bowl, jar, or pitcher, thank the sun for all it has given you. Focus on yourself as a seed primed to grow, and meditate on all the good you're planning on doing.
5. You can let the glass container steep in the sun all day (sealed) or boil and strain the tea to drink immediately.

## WORDS OF WISDOM

IF IT IS COLD OUTSIDE, FIND A WINDOW THAT FACES BOTH TOWARD THE EQUATOR AND THE SUNRISE, IF POSSIBLE.

Whether a morning person or a night owl, people can draw their strength from different points in the day. Is it natural for you to wake up early? What about the dawn is exciting or uninspiring to you? What comforts do you draw from being up late at night?

Use the sun to channel your energy into new growth. Write about new hopes and dreams, a fascinating new feeling you want to explore, or a new endeavor you plan to embark on.

Most cultures have a god of the sun. You can also invoke Helios, Xu Kai, Amun, or any other sun god of your choosing. They may be old, but they still listen. Research and write about your deity of choice.

# OPENING YOUR THIRD EYE

This spell needs time and space. To open your third eye, you first have to be in tune with all of your other senses, but this isn't as simple as just experiencing them. No, for your third eye to open, you need to exercise the existing senses.

## MATERIALS

- *Pen or pencil*
- *Paper*

## PROCESS

1. To put your senses to the test, wander to a new location. Open your heart to new experiences and break yourself out of your normal routines. Take an afternoon to wander and truly give yourself over to your senses.
2. Find new things to observe. Comb over them for every unique detail, like you're a painter and you need to memorize every detail.
3. Close your eyes and open your ears. Listen to the first layer of sounds, and then focus on the subtler background sounds. Do you hear something off in the underbrush? Is that music being carried by the breeze? Follow it and see how you interact in the soundscape.
4. Follow your nose. Find sweet-smelling flowers and baked goods and other things that delight you. Go out into nature and see if you can pick apart all of the distinct aromas in the wild.
5. Try a new food and savor each bite. Chew slowly, too, and name each sensation as it dances across your tongue. What is the texture? Does this new dish tell a story?
6. Touch soft things. Feel the story in between the grooves and knots in tree bark. Reach out and really feel things. Turn things over in your fingers. Experiment with peculiar body movements and feel how the air moves around your body.

7. Write about the new ways you experienced your old senses on the next couple of pages.
8. Find somewhere quiet to meditate. Scan your body, from the tips of your toes up to your third eye (which is between your eyebrows), and based on your work with your physical senses, try to see the world without the senses you just explored. Spend at least 10 minutes sitting still and processing your thoughts. Breathe deeply and evenly.

## WORDS OF WISDOM

THE THIRD EYE IS SLOW TO WAKE UP, BUT IT IS THE SEAT OF YOUR INTUITION AND IS ALWAYS THERE, EVEN IF IT'S A BIT GROGGY. HAVE PATIENCE.

Sight

Hearing

Smell

Taste

Touch

Third Eye

# THIRD QUARTER MOON RITUAL FOR DIPLOMACY

If you're having issues broaching difficult topics or need to be on your A game for a negotiation of some sort, this ritual calls for a natural balance of the heavens and Earth, to find a diplomatic solution to balancing power dynamics until the next quarter moon. During the full moon, charge your seven pieces of white crystal in the moonlight. Since this is a moon spell, moonstones will bring the most energy to this spell.

## MATERIALS

- *Seven pieces of white crystal*
- *Sage leaves (dried or fresh)*

## PROCESS

1. At midnight, when it is the third quarter moon, make a circle outside on solid ground with the crystals. If inside, create a circle where the crystals won't be disturbed.
2. If the weather is warm, do this without shoes on to promote grounding and connectivity. Root down into the soil and tilt your head up to the moon.
3. Dig small holes in the shape of a circle for each of the seven stones and bury them in the dirt.
4. Walk around the circle, clockwise, seven times, sprinkling handfuls of the sage leaves as you go.
5. During the waning crescent moon, new moon, and waxing crescent moon that immediately follow, return to your circle with intention by either meditating or journaling in it, or walking in a clockwise circle around it and sprinkling new dried sage leaves.
6. Begin whatever conversation or negotiation that requires diplomacy during this time, if possible. If not, continue the ritual until the discussion begins.
7. The ritual is complete once you've reached an agreement (for better or worse). Dig up the crystals, wash them, and recharge them in the light of the next full moon.

Write a first draft of the difficult conversation topic or the negotiation. Argue your side.

Repeat the previous prompt, but employ empathy to your counterpart. Argue the opposing side.

Conflict gets a bad reputation, but it is through conflict and discussion that we grow as individuals. How do you hope to grow from this diplomatic endeavor?

# MANIFESTATION & MONEY

# MONEY MAGIC FLOOR WASH

Rather than having a broom to ride on at night, this spell sweeps out the bad and washes in the new. Some of the materials are difficult to come by and that is intentional—the effort you put into a spell comes back to you threefold. Important to note: Putting yourself into debt to manifest wealth is NOT the process for a wise witch. Spend responsibly and find creative replacements, and the magic will come.

## MATERIALS

- *¼ cup (60 ml) collected rainwater*
- *¼ cup (60 ml) rosewater*
- *Pot*
- *1 sprig cedar*
- *1 stick cinnamon*
- *Any combination of the following essential oils: bergamot, geranium, neroli, rose, rosemary, and sandalwood*
- *8-ounce (240 ml) glass Mason jar with a lid*
- *Broom*
- *Dustpan*

## PROCESS

1. Combine the rainwater and rosewater in a pot and bring to a boil. Once boiling, add the cedar and cinnamon and let simmer for 3 minutes. Remove from the heat.
2. Add eight drops each of the essential oils of your choice to the pot.
3. Once the potion has cooled, transfer it to the Mason jar and seal the lid. Let it sit for 24 hours.
4. After the 24 hours have passed, start sweeping from the farthest corner of your domicile toward the front door or main entryway. This expels any bad energy that may be hiding in the corners of your home. Sweep the debris into a dustpan and immediately remove it from your house.

5. Prepare whatever method you use to wash your hard floors (Swiffer, mop, steamer, bucket and brush, etc.). These floors may only be your kitchen and bathroom, and that's okay.
6. Vigorously shake the potion in the jar and liberally sprinkle the potion on the floor (do not soak the floor).
7. Focus on cleaning the grime. Make sure you get every nook and cranny.
8. When you're done and your home smells amazing, try to associate success and valuable resources (time, energy, finances, etc.) with that smell. Channel the same focus to whatever project you are working on to bring in more funds.

## WORDS OF WISDOM

THE POTION CAN ALSO BE USED AS A REFRESHING ROOM SPRAY.

What does success mean to you? Is it having money? Receiving praise? Define what success means for you and what having success does for you.

Magic does not bring money into the fold, but it can help open your eyes to new opportunities. Seek out new opportunities to grow your wealth, community, or professional success and write about your experiences below.

Sometimes wealth doesn't come in the form of finances. What resources do you have in your arsenal that you might be overlooking in your quest for financial wealth?

# BACCHANALIA

Drawn from a slew of festivals celebrated by the ancient Greeks and Romans, Bacchanalia paid homage to Dionysus and Bacchus, the gods of wine, freedom, and delight. Not much is known about these wild and sacred rites of passage; however, at their core, Bacchanalia were meant to remove inhibitions and set participants free.

## MATERIALS

- *Small piece of paper (no larger than 2 x 1 inch, or 5 x 2.5 cm)*
- *Pen or pencil*
- *Fireproof pot*
- *Red candle*
- *Glass*
- *Pitcher with ¼ cup (60 ml) red grape juice or red wine*

## PROCESS

1. On the small piece of paper, write down a personal demon you're trying to exorcise, a habit that you want to quit, or anything else that may no longer serve you. It can be a few words or one symbol for a greater issue. For example, if you're trying to eat healthier but can't quit fries, you can draw a vegetable. Or if you're having financial troubles, you can draw a money symbol or a set of scales.
2. Over your pot, light the red candle and then take the piece of paper in your alternate hand and carefully light the paper over the pot. Drop the paper into the pot once it catches fire, being careful not to burn yourself. Visualize what your life would be like without whatever was on that paper holding you back.
3. Once the paper burns out, dust the ashes from the pot into the glass.
4. While visualizing what you'll replace the void with, pour the grape juice or red wine into the glass, over the remnants of what you're trying to expel.

*(continued)*

5. Hold the glass in line with your heart and sit with it for a moment before downing the liquid. If you do not want to drink the ashes, you can dispose of it in the dirt outside.
6. Hydrate with water afterward. Complete the following prompts and continue to journal about any additional feelings to complete the process.

## WORDS OF WISDOM

THIS SPELL IS ONE OF MANY "ROAD OPENERS," WHICH HELP THE CASTER WELCOME CHANGE AND NEW ENERGY INTO THEIR LIVES.

To inspire change, write about a time you did something utterly unexpected and it paid off.

In detail, write out the aspects of your life that are not helping you become your highest self. It may be an emotional process, but don't be afraid to let it out. It's much more dangerous to keep it bottled up.

# ROSE OF JERICHO

The rose of Jericho is an extremely resilient tumbleweed. It lightly rolls through the desert as a tight ball when it's dehydrated, and once it hits water, it unfurls into a lush, green plant.

## MATERIALS

- *Purified water*
- *Silver dollar (or other symbolic silver piece)*
- *Wide-rimmed bowl*
- *Rose of Jericho*

## PROCESS

1. If necessary, let the purified water sit in a pitcher until it reaches room temperature.
2. Place the silver dollar at the bottom of the wide-rimmed bowl. Leave it in the bowl for as long as the rose is in bloom.
3. In both hands, cradle the rose of Jericho to your heart and detail in your mind all the joy, happiness, and resources that you are trying to welcome into your life with this spell.
4. Set the rose of Jericho atop the silver dollar.
5. Slowly pour the water over the rose. If it feels right, talk to the rose while you do so. Over the next several hours the rose will open. It's a slow process, so if you want to do something in the interim, you're more than welcome to do so. If you find yourself drawn back to the rose, say sweet things to it that you would also enjoy hearing.
6. Your rose can be open for however long you'd like. If you keep it lush and green for an extended period of time, make sure to drain the water, rinse the leaves to prevent unwanted growth or mold, and refill the water to just enough to keep the bottom wet without waterlogging the plant, between ½ and 2 inches (1 and 5 cm) of water.

*(continued)*

7. Once you've reached a milestone in your manifestation, drain the water and place an offering (a single small crystal, the silver dollar from earlier, or a piece of jewelry) into the center of the plant. Leave your offering there as you wait for the rose to desiccate. This process will take several days to completely dry out, so be patient.
8. When you have completed your goal, water your rose of Jericho again, recover your offering, and give thanks.

## WORDS OF WISDOM

FOR MONEY, A SILVER DOLLAR WORKS BEST. IF YOU'RE TRYING TO MANIFEST OTHER THINGS, CRYSTALS (NON-WATER-SOLUBLE) CAN BE USED FOR GROUNDING, AND FINE SILVER JEWELRY CAN BE USED TO MANIFEST PLEASURABLE EXPERIENCES. CHOOSE YOUR OFFERING THOUGHTFULLY FOR BEST RESULTS.

Details are important when manifesting goals. If you're unsure of what you want, use this page to detail the perfect day. What is your morning routine? Who do you see during the day? How would you spend your time? Let yourself daydream so that you can manifest it into a reality.

While your rose is dried out, notice the gifts it has bestowed upon you. What are you grateful for in your life that makes you ambitious for more? How are things subtly changing now that you want to bring more of what brings you joy into the universe?

Once the rose is in bloom for the second time (when you retrieve your offering), look at the previous two entries. Has what you wanted changed over time? How do you feel now that you've manifested good into the world?

# GROWTH & LOSS

# BREAKING BAD HABITS

Sometimes the most stubborn, angry, or darkest parts of us need to be heard and felt to be let out and truly exorcised. Catharsis can be a satisfying resolution to most conflicts. Sometimes when you feel like you're going to burst, the only way to get over it is with a bit of harmless destruction.

## MATERIALS

- *Permanent marker or ink*
- *Egg(s)*
- *Pinch of salt*
- *Pitcher of distilled water*

## PROCESS

1. On page 115, write out all the bad energy you're trying to expel.
2. After you write down everything, underline, highlight, or bold the words or phrases that stand out to you the most.
3. Write these words/phrases on an egg with the marker or ink. Whisper things to the egg; they can be things you want to let go of, like regrets or anger that haunts you.
4. Add the salt to the pitcher of water and bring the pitcher to a secluded space with a hard surface.
5. Hold your egg close to your chest. Feel those feelings one final time.
6. Cast the egg against a rock or wall. Repeat this step as many times as necessary, and once you're done, wash away the yolk and shell remnants with the saltwater.

## WORDS OF WISDOM

THIS PRACTICE EXTRACTS ANYTHING THAT WOULD BE BETTER SERVED OUTSIDE YOUR CELESTIAL BODY. DO NOT DIRECT THE WORDS OR EGGS TOWARD ANY LIVING PERSON OR CREATURE, AND MAKE SURE YOU CLEAN UP AFTER YOUR CRAFT SO AS NOT TO ATTRACT PESTILENCE.

Write out all the bad energy you're trying to expel on this page. Highlight the words or phrases that stand out to you the most and write them on an egg before letting them go.

Repurpose the highlighted words into a second exercise of healing. Write down their inverse words here and meditate on how these (theoretically) positive words can be put into action.

Was there a specific person or situation that led you to these feelings? In a letter, explain how they made you feel. Be truthful and allow yourself to write without barriers.

# BURNING BROKEN BRIDGES

Closure is sometimes difficult to find. Cutting ties can be the healthiest option for relationships, but without closure, the process can feel incomplete. This is a symbolic spell to help cut any lingering strands. This spell can be for ex-friends and -significant others alike.

## MATERIALS

- *Pen*
- *Paper*
- *Photos, letters, or a piece of paper with the person's name written on it*
- *Fireproof pot and a white candle or a firepit*
- *Pinch of salt*
- *Pitcher of purified water*

## PROCESS

1. This ritual is best performed outside in the light of the new moon, but before you light any fire, write a goodbye letter on page 120 to the person that you're trying to let go of.
2. Bring all the materials outside, including the letter.
3. There are different ways to manipulate fire depending on whether you're using a candle in a pot or a firepit, but for each, the process is essentially the same. Rip off a piece of your letter, hold it to you, and say out loud something the other person did that you are better off without.
4. Light the piece of your letter on fire, being careful not to burn yourself, and let the paper go as you feel yourself letting this individual go. If using the candle and the pot, light the candle inside the pot and drop the smoldering pieces of paper into the pot. If lighting a fire in a firepit, crumple the piece of paper and throw it into the fire. Be careful of smoldering ashes.
5. Repeat the process of tearing, lighting, and letting go (or crumpling and throwing) as many times as you need with the photos and letters. It is

okay if you do not want to dispose of these vestiges. They are a part of you as much as they are a part of the other person and it is okay to want to keep some things for yourself.

6. As the remnants of your memento burn, sprinkle the salt into the pitcher of water. When you are good and thoroughly done letting go, snuff the candle and sprinkle the ashes into the breeze.
7. Pour the saltwater over the ashes and let yourself feel a release. If using a firepit, spread the pieces of wood and burning coals so that the heat is evenly distributed. Pour the pitcher of saltwater over it, making sure all the pieces are extinguished before leaving the firepit.

## WORDS OF WISDOM

ALWAYS BE CAREFUL WHEN USING FIRE IN MAGIC. IT IS POWERFUL, BUT POWER CAN GET OUT OF CONTROL. PRACTICE SAFE SPELLCRAFT AND ONLY TRY TO MANIPULATE YOUR FEELINGS, NEVER THE FEELINGS OF OTHERS.

Draft your goodbye letter here. Letting go of someone is hard and it may take a couple tries to pen a fulfilling letter. Be patient and let every part of you mourn the loss of this individual. Rewrite and refine on a separate piece of paper for the spell.

Good boundaries make for better friends. What boundaries did this individual help you discover and how can you advocate for yourself in the future?

Take some time and solitude to really root into yourself after burning this bridge. What are some things that you couldn't do with this individual that make your heart sing?

# FEAR CHEST FOR FRIENDS

Big magic is done best with a coven. A coven can be just two people, and the art of practicing together can draw friends even closer. This spell practices the difficult art of vulnerability. Many spells help bolster strength or fortitude, but this spell is to help you grow through letting yourself feel scared or afraid in a controlled setting with someone there to support you.

## MATERIALS

- *Chalk*
- *Blue candle*
- *Pen and paper*
- *Small symbolic totems*
- *2 small wooden boxes (or enough for everyone participating)*
- *Permanent marker*
- *2 pieces pink ribbon or string (or enough for everyone participating)*

## PROCESS

1. Start thinking about what you want this chest to hold a couple of days before the ritual and gather small things to put in your fear chest. If you're afraid of the dark, it could be an obsidian stone. If you're afraid of clowns, it could be a red nose. If you're afraid of being left behind, it could be a single sock or glove.
2. To begin the ritual, use the chalk to draw a white circle on the ground that is big enough for everyone participating in the ritual to sit inside of.
3. Place the blue candle in the center of the circle and light it. Take time, together, to quietly write about the things that you are most afraid of. They could be tangible things like spiders and heights or they could be deep-seated fears like abandonment and failure.
4. When everyone is done writing, go around the circle and let people talk about their fears in detail or in general terms or let them abstain from telling anything at all. The beauty of this chest is that you're trusting another person with your fears, even if you might not be able to verbally express them just yet.

*(continued)*

5. Place your totems in the box, along with the letter, and shut the box.
6. Use the marker to draw what keeps these monsters at bay on the outside of the box. For example, if you are prone to seasonal affective disorder, draw the sun. You could also draw little things that make you happy, like a bicycle if you enjoy riding your bike or a pet that lifts your spirit when you are feeling down.
7. Give your box to another person in the circle to keep. As you exchange boxes, make eye contact and express gratitude for the space to be vulnerable. Accept another's fear chest in turn and thank them for their openness and honesty.
8. Tie the pink (the color for lighthearted love and healing) ribbons or string around the boxes to help rein in your friend's demons.
9. Keep the box somewhere safe but out of the way until one or both of you are ready to face your demons.

## WORDS OF WISDOM

SAFE SPELLCRAFT IS ALWAYS CONSENSUAL. MAKE SURE YOU DISCUSS THIS SPELL BEFOREHAND WITH THE PERSON YOU'RE PREFORMING IT WITH SO THAT THEY ARE EMOTIONALLY PREPARED.

What is the root of your fear? Where does it come from? What about it makes your inner child feel unsafe?

Connection can be difficult when who we want to be isn't currently who we are. What are some ways that you can regularly practice vulnerability without opening yourself up to harm?

How did being honest about your fears with another human being make you feel?

# CONNECTION & LOVE

# WELCOMING BENEVOLENT SPIRITS INTO YOUR HOME

Spirits are all around us. They're curious and have various reasons for being. Benevolent spirits enjoy sweet smells and open channels. Here are a few ways to cleanse your house and bring some of these well-meaning spirits inside.

## MATERIALS

- *Large bouquet of sweet-smelling flowers*
- *Your favorite essential oil(s)*
- *White cloth*
- *Sweet grass, palo santo, or a smudge stick*
- *Jasmine tea*
- *Sweet-smelling incense*

## PROCESS

1. On the day of the ritual, source the bouquet of flowers. If you have a garden of your own, cut the flowers at dusk and bring them into your home.
2. Liberally drop the essential oil onto the cloth so that the oil smells strongly. Wipe down the insides of all the windows in your home, starting with the most west-facing window. Repeat for all your other windows, methodically working your way around your house until you return to your west-facing window.
3. Wipe down the outside of your front and back doors. Make sure you anoint all four sides of the entryway.
4. Go outside and light your smudging device. Wave it in the air. If it can catch a breeze and travel, even better.
5. While it's still lit, walk back inside your home and take a tour of all your rooms.
6. Once the smudge burns out, pour yourself a cup of jasmine tea (a tea to increase psychic abilities) and light the incense. Sit quietly, with your eyes closed, and open your senses to any auxiliary sounds or sensations.

What kind of spirit are you hoping to attract?

How does having a clean space that smells good impact your mood and the things that you want to do?

Everyone has a ghost story; share yours.

# WITCH MIRROR FOR DIVINATION

A witch mirror is a divine way to connect with yourself and reflect on your relationship with others. The art of making a witch mirror is a personal act that in turn not only helps you see the future, but also makes you an intrinsic part of its telling.

## MATERIALS

- *3 cups (700 ml) mugwort, jasmine, or dandelion tea*
- *Handheld compact mirror*
- *Black acrylic paint or black nail polish*
- *White acrylic paint or white nail polish*
- *Pen or pencil*
- *Paper*

## PROCESS

1. Brew your first cup of tea. Set it on your altar and drink it slowly as you work.
2. While you drink your tea, vertically paint half of your mirror with the black paint. It can be smooth, ridged, goopy, swirling, abstract, or include symbols. Make sure you ONLY paint half of the mirror.
3. Refill your cup of tea and return to your altar to paint the other half of the mirror white. You can employ the same technique you used for the black side or it can be different. Follow your flow and allow yourself to really fall into your task.
4. Let the mirror sit out on your altar to dry. Depending on how much paint you used, this may take some time.
5. When you return to your witch mirror, come back with a third and final cup of tea. Before you look at it, bring an open-ended question to your mind. "Yes" or "no" answers usually do not translate in divination.
6. With the question at the forefront of your mind and your consciousness focused on your third eye, observe the black side of the mirror with a soft gaze.

Let your vision swim and pull out abstract images. What jumps out at you? Record your impressions on page 136.

7. Once you're done with the black side, close your eyes, take a deep breath, and repeat the process for the white side. Let your mind open. What do you see here? Write it down in a stream of consciousness on page 137.

## WORDS OF WISDOM

DIVINATION IS BEST USED WHEN YOU'RE BLOCKED, CONFUSED, OR NEED TO MAKE A DECISION WITH GREATER CONFIDENCE THAN YOU CURRENTLY HAVE. KEEP IN MIND THAT OUTSIDE SOURCES CAN GUIDE YOU, BUT IN THE END, THIS IS YOUR JOURNEY AND YOU SHOULD BE THE MAIN PERSON MAKING DECISIONS.

What imagery jumped out at you from the black side of the witch mirror?

What did you see in the white side of the witch mirror that called to you?

Light and dark are often paired as moral judgments on “good” and “bad.” But our sweetest dreams come during the night, and fire carries with it the ability to burn. How do you interpret black and white in divination? Was there any gray?

# WITCH BOTTLE FOR PROTECTION

Spells sealed in glass jars or bottles are great for altar spaces, home and hearth, or to take with you on the move (if they're small and portable enough). They can be in Mason jars, old wine bottles, upcycled herb jars, or small bottles with corks. Create a safe, stress-free space for yourself with this bottle of protection.

## MATERIALS

- *Small glass jar or bottle*
- *Small piece of paper*
- *Pen or pencil*
- *Dried bay leaves*
- *Dried rosemary*
- *Small tiger's eye or jasper crystal*
- *Dried sage*
- *Dried basil*
- *Pink sea salt*
- *Tray (to catch the wax)*
- *Candle or sealing wax (white)*
- *Twine or string (black or red)*

## PROCESS

1. Clean your glass jar or bottle with hot water and soap. Dry it so it shines clear and no moisture remains.
2. On the piece of paper, write your intention for the spell and what you think you need protection from. The paper should be small enough to fit inside your jar or bottle when rolled into a tight coil. Add it to the witch bottle.
3. The herbs and crystals listed above have strong associations with protective magic. Smell them and add them to your jar or bottle as you see fit. The most visually dynamic way would be to layer them, but mixing them all together can inspire their magical powers to complement one another.

*(continued)*

4. Close your jar or bottle and place it on the tray. Light the candle or sealing wax and tilt it over the opening of the jar or bottle and let the wax drip over the cap or lid. Cover the cap or lid so it is truly sealed.
5. Let the wax dry, usually no longer than 30 minutes, and then take your black or red twine or string and bind the spell by wrapping it at least three times around the neck of the bottle or right below the wax cap of the jar. If you'd like to add an additional charm (such as a crystal, charm from a charm bracelet, piece of sea glass, or anything else that sings to you) to the twine or string, now would be the time to do it.
6. Place your witch bottle somewhere in your kitchen or hearth for protection of the home or carry it with you for protection on the go.

## WORDS OF WISDOM

USE YOUR INTUITION TO SEE WHICH HERBS AND CRYSTALS CALL OUT TO YOU.

Feeling safe and protected fosters a whole host of benefits. Stress chemically changes our bodies, and when we're constantly in fight-or-flight mode, we do not perform at our highest potential. What are some stressors that chronically plague your best self?

Rosemary and sage are strong protective herbs and elicit a pungent smell. Pinch some of the leaves between your index finger and thumb to release their aroma. What memories do they recall and what emotions do you tie to them?

Write about the last safe space you had. What made it feel so welcoming, and how did you prosper because of it?

First published in 2020 by Rock Point, an imprint of The Quarto Group,
142 West 36th Street, 4th Floor, New York, NY 10018, USA
T (212) 779-4972 F (212) 779-6058 www.QuartoKnows.com



10 9 8 7 6 5 4 3 2 1

ISBN: 978-1-63106-733-4

Publisher: Rage Kindelsperger
Creative Director: Laura Drew
Managing Editor: Cara Donaldson
Senior Editor: Erin Canning
Text: Leeann Moreau
Art Director: Cindy Samargia Laun
Interior Design: Silverglass



Printed in China